Top: Library writing table (*Osterley Park, Middlesex*) and a Serpentine commode (*The Lady Lever Art Gallery*).

THE
BOOK OF
ENGLISH FURNITURE

Edward T. Joy

SOUTH BRUNSWICK
NEW YORK: A. S. BARNES AND CO.

11/30/66 Eastern 3.80

© *Edward T. Joy, 1964*

Library of Congress Catalogue Card Number: 65-24845

A. S. Barnes and Co., Inc.
South Brunswick, New Jersey

6278

Printed in the United States of America

Contents

List of Plates

The Victorian Period

The Twentieth Century

LINE DRAWINGS IN TEXT

ACKNOWLEDGMENTS

The author wishes to express his gratitude to the following for their generous help with the illustrations (a large number of which are appearing for the first time) and for much valuable advice:

Norman Adams Ltd; Plates 27, 31, 35, 50, 51, 52, 54, 55, 62, 69, 70, 71, 72, 73, 74, 77, 82, 90, 93, 94, 96, 97, 98.

Michael Barnes, Esq.: Figures 1, 2, 3, 4, 5, 6, 7, 8, 9.

Edward Barnsley, Esq.: Plates 132, 133, 134, 135.

H. Blairman & Sons Ltd: Plates 95, 99, 100.

Country Life Ltd.: Frontispiece, Plate 103.

Messrs Heal's of Tottenham Court Road, London: Plates 120, 121, 122, 123, 124, 125.

Hotspur Ltd: Plates 17, 18, 24, 32, 33, 39, 40, 41, 42, 43, 44, 46, 53, 56, 57, 58, 59, 60, 64, 65, 66, 67, 75, 76, 79, 80, 84, 85, 86, 87, 88, 89.

Mrs Wallace Hughes: Plate 106.

H. W. Keil Ltd: Plates 10, 19, 20, 21, 23, 25, 26, 29.

Alan Peters, Esq.: Plate 136

Phillips of Hitchin, Ltd: Plates 28, 30, 34, 36, 45, 48, 49, 61, 63, 68, 78, 81, 83.

Gordon Russell Ltd: Plates 126, 127, 128, 129, 130, 131.

S. W. Wolsey Ltd: Plates 1, 2, 3, 4, 5, 6, 7, 8, 9, 11, 12, 13, 14, 15, 16, 22.

Temple Williams Ltd: Plates 91, 92

J. Barbee Winston, Esq., New Orleans, U.S.A.: Plates 37, 38, 47 (from his collection of early mahogany furniture).

Victoria and Albert Museum: Plates 108, 109, 110, 111, 113, 114, 115, 116, 117, 118, 119.

Bruce Whineray, Esq.: Plates 101, 102, 104, 105, 107, 112.

Introduction

This book traces the development of English furniture from 1500 to the present day. The problems facing the designers and makers of furniture (often, but not necessarily, the same men), and their success or failure in solving them, must always be related to the social conditions of the craftsmen's times, and to the materials and techniques at their command. Both these points have been considered in this survey, and brief explanations have been made of developments in construction and decoration.

It will be noticed that although English craftsmen have always been quick to absorb foreign influences (just as foreign craftsmen have borrowed from us), their traditional approach has been to use the most suitable materials and methods in a direct way. For this reason, to stop this survey short at 1830, the accepted limit for antique furniture, would be to miss many interesting subsequent developments, such as the revival of craftsmanship in the period of the Arts and Crafts Movement (when English furniture was admired throughout Europe), and the struggle to achieve good design in the greatly changed conditions of the 20th century.

In fact, a study of antique furniture is given even more value if the appreciation of design and skill which it encourages can be applied dispassionately to the consideration of modern furniture, whose designers, after all, face very much the same problems as did their predecessors.

For the interest and information of readers, I have included, as Appendices, a glossary of technical and decorative terms pertaining to furniture, and glossaries of woods used in furniture-making (a) prior to 1830 and (b) from 1830 onwards.

Oak Furniture: *c.*1500-1660

The 'age of oak' is the traditional name for the period from early medieval times to *c.* 1660 when this timber was the principal material for furniture. The wood was converted by first felling and quartering the trunk (i.e., splitting it along its length into four sections), then cutting each quarter towards the centre, along the lines of the medullary rays, which produce the characteristic silver grain or figure of oak, and make it more durable and less inclined to warp (Fig. 1). Until the later

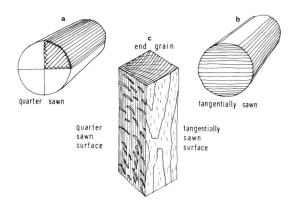

Fig. 1. How furniture wood is sawn. (*a*) Quarter sawn, (*b*) tangentially sawn, (*c*) quarter sawn surface.

Tudor period it was usual to split the log with beetle and wedge, and to trim the riven wood with the adze; the later method was to have the wood sawn across the top of a saw-pit by two men, the top and bottom sawyer, operating a large two-handed saw above and below the log.

In spite of great care taken over seasoning, oak was still liable to move in the atmosphere. In early oak pieces such as boarded chests (which were composed of six boards), the planks were fastened together by nails or oak pins, a method which persisted in country areas until the 18th century. But pinning allowed no freedom of movement in the wood, which often split across the grain. To remedy this, the panel and frame construction was used for chests, chairs and doored furniture. Oak panels were tapered on all sides to fit into deep, narrow grooves in a rectangular framework composed of horizontal rails and vertical stiles. These were united by the mortise and tenon joint, a projecting

Fig. 2. Panelled chest construction.

1. Oak boarded chest decorated with 'chip' carving; there are traces of polychrome decoration. Late 15th century.

section (the tenon) of the rail being fitted into a corresponding socket (the mortise) of the stile, and secured by squared and tapered oak pegs driven through round holes (Fig. 2). The panel now had sufficient room to move and so was much less liable to warp.

This method, introduced into England from Flanders in the 15th century, amounted to a technical revolution. 'Joined' furniture now made by the joiner was lighter, stronger and better proportioned than that made previously by the carpenter.

Early Tudor, 1485–1558. Early Tudor furniture retained many of the characteristics of the furniture made in the Middle Ages, when it was designed to be carted about from place to place as its owners—king, barons, churchmen—moved about the country. It was largely the exclusive possession of the rich, who at first were slow to absorb the new ideas of the Renaissance and to adapt themselves to the increased opportunities for domestic comfort. Thus movable pieces like chests, folding chairs, stools, benches and trestle tables were prominent in large houses where social life still centred in the

2. Early Tudor oak trestle stool.

3. Early 16th-century oak bench.

4. Early Tudor oak chair; back carved with medallioned head in profile.

5. Oak trestle dining table. Early 16th century.

great hall. Much of the best furniture, however, was imported, or made in England by foreign joiners.

The chest was the most important medieval piece, for it could be used as a seat, bed or table as well as for storage and transport. Boarded chests, of the early type of six boards nailed or pinned together (Plate 1), were still being made with, however, thinner boards, about three quarters of an inch thick. Another type of chest, of the kind made since the 13th century, had the front and back made of three planks, the central one being framed and pegged into grooves in the other two, which were lengthened to form feet. The panelled chest (Plate 12) was only gradually adopted, and was comparatively rare until Queen Elizabeth I's reign. Other varieties of chest were the hutch, a box-like receptacle with doors on legs, the standard, a large travelling chest and the coffer, of smaller size. The best coffers were made by cofferers, who covered them with leather and other valuable materials, and also made and covered other pieces of furniture.

Throughout the Tudor period stools, forms (or benches) (Plates 2, 3) and settles (i.e., forms with arms and backs) were the usual seats; 'stool', in fact, was the normal term for a seat for one person. Chairs (Plate 4), comparatively rare pieces, were symbols of authority and reserved for the heads of households or for distinguished guests. Joined chairs had panelled backs, seats and arms; 'X chairs' were often covered with rich materials and found only in great houses; turned (or 'thrown') chairs were made by turners and had triangular seats and legs, arms, backs and supports formed of turned members. 'Thrown' work by turners was distinct from 'joined' work, as turners did not use the mortise and tenon joint, but fitted the ends of turned sections into sockets.

A newer kind of lighter panelled chair, the caquetoire (or caqueteuse), had a narrow panelled back and was open under the seat and arms; it was intended for parlours and bedrooms and was based on French originals.

Trestle tables—boards (or tops) on trestle supports—of medieval type continued to be made (Plate 5). Some trestles were kept in position by one or two stretchers (i.e., cross-rails) which passed through the trestles and were fastened outside them by oak wedges. These wedges could easily be removed and the trestles stored away. The table tops or boards were massive planks secured by

6. Elizabethan draw table with bulb supports of 'cup and cover' form; frieze decorated with guilloches.

battens on the under side. But an indication of more settled social conditions was the growing use of the joined table (or table dormant), with its top fixed permanently to the underframing, and its legs connected by stretchers just above ground level.

More convenient still was the draw table, which made its appearance about 1550. A small plank was fixed across the centre of the underframe of the table, and on each side were the two smaller draw-leaves which lay, when the table was closed, under the main table top. Each draw-leaf pulled out on two runners fixed in slots in the table frame; these runners were so sloped that the extended draw-leaf came to rest level with the main table top, and they also had small blocks on them which rested against the table frame to prevent the leaves coming out too far. This draw-leaf principle, by which the table top can be extended to almost double its length, is still used today in table construction (Plate 6).

'Cupboards' mentioned in early Tudor inventories were not the doored structures as now understood, for in its original meaning a 'cup-board' was a table or shelf for displaying the family plate to visitors. But it seems clear that sections at least of some of these open shelves were enclosed, for there are references to 'close cupboards' and 'cupboards with aumbries'. An aumbry was an old term for any space enclosed by a door or for a doored compartment in a larger piece of furniture; it also came to mean a doored receptacle in which the almoner of a great house kept broken meats to distribute to the poor. By 1500 such houses also had food cupboards, with doors pierced for ventilation, and livery cupboards for storing the food and drink delivered daily to retainers, though there is no certain evidence that these latter cupboards had doors.

There were, in addition, hall and parlour cupboards in two stages, sometimes only the upper stage, sometimes both stages, being enclosed (the completely enclosed type is now referred to as a 'press cupboard', Plate 11); and presses, tall doored pieces containing shelves for clothes and linen. But it is important to note that 'cupboard' did not have its modern sense until the end of the Tudor period (Plate 7).

The bed was the most valuable piece of furniture on account of its costly hangings and bedding,

7. Open tiered oak 'cup-board' with canted sides.

8. Early Tudor bed with elaborately carved head board and foot posts; illustrated by Henry Shaw in *Specimens of Ancient Furniture* (1836).

9. Elizabethan walnut armchair, decorated with inlay.

which covered the plain wooden framework. Until the early 16th century the hangings were suspended from a canopy of rich material which was attached to the ceiling by cords. Then four corner posts came into use, with a panelled head board (Plate 8). It seems that the suspended canopy was retained until it was replaced, about 1550, by a wooden tester resting on the posts.

There is evidence that from medieval times until 1550 furniture was painted both to preserve the wood and to brighten the interior. Carved ornament was rich but somewhat coarsely executed, and often showed an incongruous mixture of traditional and Renaissance motives, the latter having been introduced under Henry VIII by Italian craftsmen. Panels were carved with Gothic tracery and 'linenfold' patterns, as well as with profile medallioned heads, vases, scrolls and other attempts at classical decoration. Much ornament took the form of shallow 'chip' carving with chisel and gouge (Plate 1).

Late Tudor or Elizabethan, 1558–1603. The vigour of national life in Elizabeth I's reign was reflected in the ostentatious decoration of its furniture, just as its growing wealth was reflected in the greater variety of furniture now found in the large houses being built or renovated with more comfortable interiors. In new houses, which no longer had defence as the prime consideration, the great hall was replaced by the great chamber, long gallery and more private rooms for the family.

After the Reformation the tenuous links with Italy were severed, and the Renaissance reached England in its florid Flemish and German versions, made widely familiar through imported pattern books of printed designs. The most characteristic decorative features were strapwork (i.e., arabesques and geometrical interlacing), arcading, chequer and floral inlay, and elaborate 'bulbs' (Plates 6, 10). Inlay was done by cutting the required pattern from the ground to a depth of about an eighth of an inch and fitting in pieces of wood of similar pattern and contrasting colours. For this purpose coloured woods were employed, including holly, bog oak, sycamore, poplar, beech, ash, yew and fruit woods. The 'bulbs', which had obvious resemblances to the puffed sleeves and trunks of Elizabethan costume, were built up by gluing sections to a central post on cupboard supports, bedposts, legs of dining tables, etc. They often had an Ionic capital at the top and were divided by a moulding into a 'cup and cover' form (Plate 6).

10. Oak splay-fronted cupboard with lion and bulb supports, decorated with inlay, split balusters, gadrooning and lunettes. Early 17th century.

11. Press cupboard with lozenge decoration on the panels, and lunettes on the frieze.

12. Oak panelled chest, decorated with carved arcading, guilloches (on the stiles) and lozenge ornament (on the sides). Early 17th century.

The growing use of glass windows led to the abandonment of the old custom of painting furniture, which was now inlaid with varied coloured woods, or upholstered (in the case of seats), or waxed and varnished. The search for colour led to the use of imported tapestries and carpets for wall coverings, and of rich materials for upholstery. Joiners were now using more woods, including walnut, chestnut, birch and cedar.

Joined chairs with panelled backs were made in greater numbers towards the end of the century. They became lighter and more open, losing the panel beneath the seat and arms (Plate 9). The front legs were turned in baluster shapes (i.e., like columns) and continued upwards to support the arms; back legs remained rectangular in section. Many chairs were inlaid with coloured woods. By 1600 the top rail, instead of being tenoned between the uprights, began to extend above them, with brackets ('ears') added at the sides. Richly upholstered seating furniture was also becoming more plentiful, the upholstery in some cases covering the softwood framework.

After 1550 joined stools with four turned legs began to replace the type with solid splayed ends; these legs, which were joined to deep rails beneath the seat, and to stretcher rails just above floor level, straddled outwards. Stools and benches were often made in sets to go with a table.

For about a century after 1550 two types of cupboard were generally used for service at meals in large households. One, the court cupboard, preserved the old meaning of a stand for plate and dishes, for it consisted of three open tiers or shelves, the top two being supported at the front corners by bulbous columns. Sometimes the space above the middle shelf had a doored compartment (Plate 10). The other type (the press cupboard) (Plate 11) was larger than the court cupboard, and had two stages, the lower one having shelves enclosed by doors, the upper a shallow recessed cupboard which was sometimes splayed at the sides to give more shelf space.

Draw tables (Plate 6), long dining tables with fixed tops and six or eight legs, and side tables with four or six legs, were all richly carved. So were the great beds, heavy and ornate structures, with the tester now supported, not on four posts, but on the panelled head board and on two bulbous foot posts which stood independent of the low bed frame.

Many chests were inlaid with grotesques, animals and representations of buildings. A special kind, known as 'Nonsuch chests', were inlaid with coloured woods in the shape of a palace, said, without authority, to resemble Henry VIII's palace of Nonsuch in Surrey.

13. Small oak table with drawer; bobbin-turned legs and stretchers; carved lunette decoration on frieze. First half of 17th century.

14. Armchair, *c*.1625, with original 'Turkey work' upholstery.

Fig. 3. Drawer construction. First half 17th century. Crude dovetail.

15. Chair, Yorkshire-Derbyshire type; c.1650.

Fig. 4. Drawer construction. Second half 17th century. Also shows veneered drawer front.

Early Stuart, 1603–60. The first half of the 17th century marks the climax of the 'age of oak'. Under the patronage of James I (1603–25) and the cultured Charles I (1625–49) the architect Inigo Jones introduced true Italian architecture in the Palladian style to England, but progress in architecture, interior decoration and furniture was slowed down by Charles's quarrel with parliament. There were, nevertheless, interesting developments in chairs, chests of drawers and tables.

In James I's reign, from which the term 'Jacobean' derives, there was a tendency to tone down some of the excessive ornament of Elizabethan furniture, and 'bulbs' became more slender. There was still, however, much strapwork in low relief, floral decoration, and carving of lunettes, arcading, guilloches, etc. (Plates 12, 13). Simpler decoration became apparent under Charles I, and particularly in the Commonwealth period (1649–60), when Puritan austerity was the rule.

A decorative feature of the time was the split baluster. The member was turned to the required shape, then split down the middle; the matching pairs were usually stained black and glued to the surface of the piece (Plates 10, 15). Chests, which were still important, especially in country areas, had panelled backs and sides, and larger ones had panelled lids also. Arched panels were a characteristic of the period (Plate 12). Panel corners were mitred—i.e., each edge of the mouldings framing the panel was cut at an angle of 45°, these mouldings being run on separate pieces of oak and glued into position.

In the early years of the 17th century the best chairs of 'X frame' type had elaborate upholstery richly trimmed. Joined chairs often had arched and inlaid panels. Distinct innovations were 'back stools', the first chairs to be made without arms, among which were the so-called 'farthingale chairs', said to have been made for women wearing the fashionable farthingales (hooped skirts) of James's reign.

About 1650 appeared the type known as Yorkshire-Derbyshire chairs, which had their backs filled with two flat hooped rails, or with an arcading of balusters (Plate 15). The austerity of Cromwell's regime was reflected in the introduction of plain chairs with seats and back panels covered with leather or some other simple material, secured to the frame by brass-headed studs.

16. Table with folding top and bobbin turned legs; *c.*1650.

The chest of drawers in its earliest form appeared before 1650. Drawers, then known as 'tills' or 'drawing boxes', had been fitted to cabinets and travelling coffers from *c.*1550, and before 1600 the 'mule chest', with a single drawer at the bottom, came into use, making it much easier to reach lower layers of linen, clothing, etc. Later, two or more drawers, sometimes enclosed by doors, were placed below the box-like upper section with its hinged lid, but this hybrid type was not common until *c.* 1650 (Plate 25).

At about the same time the first true chest of drawers appeared in the form of a narrow drawer at the top, a single deep drawer beneath this, and three long drawers behind panelled doors at the base. A little later the lower doors were omitted, thus making a complete chest of drawers, but still with the deep upper drawer.

These pieces were often decorated with applied mouldings and split balusters, and inlaid with bone and mother-of-pearl. The stout oak drawer sides, which were nailed to the fronts, had grooves made in them so that they could slide along runners (or bearers) fixed to the inside framing. By 1650 the sides were joined to the front of the drawer by crude dovetails. In time the number of such dovetails increased, and they became more slender (Figs. 3, 4).

Gate-leg tables were found in many early Stuart households, developed from the oak tables with folding tops and pivoted supports which had been known since the 15th century (Plate 16). In these earlier tables one of the legs was halved vertically and framed to stretchers of half thickness so that it could swing out to support the unfolded top. In the later tables each gate was composed of two legs connected at the top and bottom by stretchers, one leg being pivoted to the table frame. The gates were swung out to support the flaps which were fastened to the fixed centre of the table by wrought iron hinges (these were nailed on until screws came into use after 1650). By means of halvings (i.e., matching sockets in the stretchers of the main framing and in the bottom of the swing-out leg) the legs could shut tight when not in use.

The Walnut Period: *c.* 1660-1750

After 1660 numbers of foreign craftsmen, particularly from the Low Countries and France (including Huguenots fleeing from religious persecution after the revocation of the Edict of Nantes in 1685) came to work in England, some of them at the court, and they passed on to English craftsmen their latest constructional techniques and decorative processes. By 1700 there was considerably more specialisation among English furniture-makers, who were now sub-divided into cabinet-makers, chair-makers, clock-case-makers, upholsterers, japanners, gilders, carvers, etc.

Veneers, Marquetry and Parquetry. From *c.*1660 to *c.*1750 the fashionable furniture wood was walnut, which is particularly associated with the technique of veneering, the process by which thin sheets of sawn wood—the veneers—were glued to the flush surface of the 'carcase', or solid frame, so that the figure of the wood could show to advantage. This new method required such careful preparation and execution that a new class of specialist craftsmen—the cabinet-makers—came into existence.

17. Long-case clock decorated with floral marquetry in various woods; *c.*1685.

18. Side table with twist-turned legs and curved flat stretchers, decorated with marquetry; *c.*1685.

19. Charles II period lacquered cabinet on carved and silvered stand.

Fig. 5. Veneer cut away to show common dovetailing.

Fig. 6. Lapped dovetail and cock beading.

Veneers were sawn to the thickness of about one-sixteenth of an inch by sawyers who went from shop to shop for the purpose. Veneers sawn from the same log repeated its figure, and successive sections of the same pattern, matched, opposed or reversed, could be laid on the carcase—across for instance, a drawer front, or on the top of a table, or from top to bottom of a chest of drawers. On large surfaces, 'quartering' (laying four veneers with the figure twice reversed) was common.

The joiners' technique of panel and frame construction did not give the flush surface that was essential for veneering, and oak was an unsuitable background for veneers, yellow deal being both more stable and cheaper. Oak, however, was used for drawer linings in veneered furniture.

The most skilled craftsmen used veneers of rich figure, or cuts taken transversely from small branches of trees (which produced oval patterns known as oyster pieces), or burr veneers which were cut from malformations on tree trunks and produced, not a regular pattern, but a tangled mass of veins. These burr veneers were difficult to cut and apply, as they tended to curl, but they gave a most attractive decoration (Plate 48). As well as walnut, other woods, if they had an interesting figure, were much sought after for veneers by cabinet-makers, such as maple, yew, elm, ash, mulberry and kingwood, and, for oyster pieces, olive and laburnum.

The decorative effect of veneered furniture was enhanced in several ways. Cross-banded borders— i.e., short strips of veneer in which the grain ran across the width (Fig. 4), with a narrow inner 'herring-bone' banding, so called because it was composed of tiny strips of veneer of contrasted colours on the slant—were generally used on larger surfaces. Drawer fronts, however, often had herring-bone banding only.

The through or common dovetail which was used on early veneered furniture exposed the end-grain and did not give a satisfactory surface for veneers; it was therefore replaced by the 'lapped' or 'stopped' dovetail, which left a lap on the pin piece (Figs. 5, 6).

Closely allied to the technique of veneering was that of marquetry, which employed veneers of

20. *Left:* Interior of lacquered cabinet showing drawer space for the collection of 'curiosities'.

21. *Above:* Chased metal hinges, corner mounts and lock-plate of lacquered cabinet; these mounts were widely copied on contemporary walnut cabinets.

coloured woods to form intricate patterns (Plates 17, 18). The required design was first drawn on paper and pricked through on to other sheets to get duplicates. The pattern was pasted on top of several layers of veneer, which were fastened with panel pins or glued together with interleaved sheets of paper. The marquetry-cutter then cut through the whole of the veneers with a fine frame saw, along the lines of the drawing. Selected pieces of the design were arranged on the veneer ground in the manner of a jig-saw puzzle.

For floral marquetry, which was fashionable until *c.*1690 (and later than 1690 on clock cases), many woods were used, suitable shades being obtained where necessary by staining, dyeing, or scorching the veneers with hot sand. But after *c.*1690 arabesque or 'seaweed' marquetry became fashionable, and for this only two woods were necessary to give the contrasted light and dark shades —walnut for the ground and either box or holly for the pattern (Plate 29). A simple geometrical type of marquetry known as parquetry was composed of a ground of oyster pieces in narrow lines of holly, box or sycamore forming circles, stars, etc. (Plate 25).

Turning. In the early walnut period, spiral or twist turning of supports was one of its outstanding features, and for some years supplanted baluster forms (Plate 18). The lathe on which the turner had hitherto worked had only been able to cut shapes at right angles to the axis of the work, but a special device now enabled it to cut obliquely, so that spirals could be turned and then finished by hand. Sometimes a double twist was made, the hollows being completely gouged out to give an open effect.

In the last quarter of the 17th century baluster turning returned to favour, and some graceful shapes were produced in William and Mary's reign, particularly 'bells' and 'pegs' (Plate 26). But after 1700 turning declined until the advent of Adam's neo-classic style of *c.*1760 (Plate 67).

Mouldings. Mouldings—the projecting bands shaped by the moulding plane to the required section —added decorative effect to cornices, friezes, plinths, edges of tables, etc., and to fronts of chests of drawers. They were covered with cross-grain veneer. Tall pieces of the later Stuart period, such as chests on stands and tallboys, were given architectural style cornices by the addition of mouldings to

22. Walnut armchair with twist-turned supports, caned seat and back, and carved royal arms, cupids and crowns. Dated 20th February, 1687/8, and inscribed 'George Lewis' (i.e., George, Elector of Hanover, later George I of England).

23. Turned walnut 'sleeping' chair with adjustable back and contemporary upholstery; *c.*1670.

24. Oak chest of drawers on stand with baluster legs; c.1690.

form either a cavetto (i.e., concave) or a swell frieze. Various mouldings were found on chests of drawers. A half round moulding was applied to the carcase surrounding the drawer front after c.1690 (Fig. 7). This was followed by the double half round moulding between 1700 and 1715 (Fig. 8). After 1710 the moulding was fixed to the edge of the drawer and projected in ovolo section to hide the line between opening and drawer when the latter was closed (Fig. 9).

Lacquer and Japanning. After 1660 much richly-coloured lacquer furniture from China and Japan was imported into England by the East India Company, including screens and panels, which were made up into pieces of furniture, and cabinets, which were mounted on carved and gilt or silvered stands (Plates 19, 20, 21). Oriental lacquer (made from the sap of the lac-tree which was not found in Europe) became so fashionable that English furniture was exported to the East to be lacquered and brought back again.

This fashion encouraged an English imitation known as japanning. Enthusiastic amateurs japanned their own furniture, particularly after the publication in 1688 of a manual, Stalker and Parker's *Treatise of Japanning and Varnishing*, while professional japanners, faced with the competition of oriental work, successfully petitioned Parliament in 1700 to curtail imports by the imposition of crippling tariffs.

For japanning, the wood was given a coating of whiting and size, and then covered with coats of coloured varnish to form the ground. The design was painted on in gilding and in colours mixed with gum-arabic. Details in relief were formed by adding a paste of gum-arabic and whiting which was coloured and gilded. A form of incised oriental lacquer known as 'Bantam work' was imitated by japanners by cutting out the design from the ground of whiting and size, then colouring and gilding

25. Chest with lift-up top and drawers below, on stand with twist-turned legs and shaped stretchers; upper stage decorated with parquetry of laburnum oyster pieces; *c*.1690.

26. Walnut settee with turned baluster ('bell') legs and waved stretchers; contemporary upholstery; *c*.1690.

Fig. 7. Half-round moulding. Fig. 8. Double half-round (reeded) moulding. Fig. 9. Ovolo lip moulding.

it. Although many pieces of furniture, including cabinets, bureaux, bookcases and mirrors, were japanned with pseudo-oriental motives, English japanning was inferior to oriental lacquer both in colour and the vitality of the designs.

Gesso. Gilt gesso furniture became fashionable under Charles II and reached its peak from 1700 to 1730. Gold leaf was applied by either water-gilding or oil-gilding to a ground of gesso, a composition of whiting and size which was laid on the wood (usually deal) in several coats and left hard and smooth. For water-gilding the gesso was covered with a special clay and wet thoroughly; the leaf had to be applied with great skill and speed, as the water dried rapidly. A second coat of gold could be applied for fine quality work, and brightly burnished.

Neither this 'double-gilding' nor burnishing was obtainable by oil-gilding, a slower, cheaper and more durable method which was commonly used after 1660. The raised decoration found on the gilt chairs, mirrors (Plate 27), side tables, picture-frames, stands and cabinets of this time was first carved in wood then glued to the surface before the composition was applied. Armorial bearings and monograms were often used in gesso work.

The Early Walnut Period: 1660-90

The Restoration of Charles II in 1660 was an important landmark in English furniture history. Inspired by the example of the king and his court, who had become used to the elegance of continental furniture and decoration during their eleven years' exile abroad, the English upper classes sought more comfort and luxury. The rebuilding of London after the Great Fire of 1666 provided a unique opportunity to stock the new houses with furniture of the latest fashion. After eleven years of Puritan domination there was an understandable swing to elaborate decoration. The famous diaries of John Evelyn and Samuel Pepys make frequent reference to luxurious living and to new and varied types of furniture.

Typical of this period were the tall-backed walnut chairs with caned seats and back panels. At first legs, stretchers and uprights were twist turned; later arms and legs were scrolled (though they did not supersede twist turning in Charles's reign). Elaborate carving decorated the cresting rails and front stretchers (which had matching motives), and the back panel frames (Plate 22). Cane was widely used on chairs as it made them lighter. Daybeds or couches, with six or more legs, had similar decoration. Stools were still widely used and followed contemporary chair styles. Upholstered armchairs and settees with wings and padded arms, covered with rich imported materials like velvet and damask, or with wool needlework on canvas, worked at home, were introduced at this time (Plate 23).

Eating-rooms now had gate-legged tables, sometimes in sets of three, two of semicircular form being joined to a central rectangular one as required. Small tables with twist turned legs united by flat stretchers (Plate 18) were used about the house for a variety of purposes, a fashionable combination being a side table with a portable candle-stand at each side, and a mirror above. As mirrors were made at Vauxhall shortly after 1660, and were no longer all imported, they came into more general use, though still expensive. These early English mirrors, with plates up to about forty-five inches in length, were mounted in broad rectangular frames of convex section decorated with veneers or marquetry (sometimes with tortoiseshell and ebony enrichments).

It was usual to mount case furniture, such as writing cabinets, cabinets, bureaux, chests and chests of drawers, on stands with twist turned (and, later, scrolled) legs (Plates 24, 25). Writing cabinets, or scrutoires, had a large fall-front. Cabinets, with folding doors, were intended to contain the valuable collections of 'curiosities' made by the rich. It was the craftsman who could make these fine cabinets and decorate them with marquetry on the doors (inside and out), and on the drawer fronts, who took the title of 'cabinet-maker'.

Another new piece was the long-case clock, in which the long pendulum greatly increased the accuracy of time-keeping and ushered in the golden age of English clock-making (Plates 17, 29, 33). The smaller bracket clocks, with handles to facilitate carriage from room to room, used the 'bob' pendulum. Domestic bookcases were also coming into fashion, the earliest recorded being those which Pepys commissioned in 1666. Beds grew higher as the height of rooms increased, and now had their wooden framework hidden by expensive materials.

27. *Opposite:* Three pieces of *c.*1725: a gilt gesso mirror; a small walnut bureau (two feet wide) with bracket feet; and a walnut chair of the Queen Anne type, with cabriole legs and claw-and-ball feet.

32. Early 18th-century mirror with flat veneered frame.

33. Long-case clock in Virginia walnut; movement by Daniel Delander; c.1725.

34. Early 18th-century walnut kneehole dressing table.

acanthus leaf or shell ornament on the knees, front seat rail and cresting. The more expensive chairs were veneered on the seat rails, splats and uprights, which were flattened for the purpose, and had four cabriole legs (unlike most chairs, which had the rear legs plain).

Settees now had lower backs and were of two main types: wide versions of upholstered chairs, or combinations of double chair form (which had been known in the early Stuart period). One version of upholstered settee for two persons has been given the modern name of 'love seat'.

Chests of drawers and bureaux acquired the forms which are still familiar and have never been bettered. One type of narrow chest of drawers (the so-called 'bachelor's chest') had a folding top for writing and seems to have been used in bedrooms. A popular piece of the early 18th century was the writing cabinet, then called 'desk and bookcase' (i.e., bureau-bookcase), the upper stage being usually faced with looking-glass plates. Many of these cabinets were of quite narrow width (under three feet), as also were bureaux and pedestal dressing tables, so that they could stand against the pier-wall—i.e., between windows, to get light from both sides. Although straight cornices were found on these bureau-bookcases, they often had arched domes and broken pediments, with gilt urn finials. Broken pediments, of straight or semicircular form, were so called from their central recess flanking a small plinth.

About 1710 the chest-on-chest or tallboy began to take the place of the chest on stand (Plate 36). The corners of the upper chest were often chamfered (as were sometimes those of the lower chest) and faced with pilasters headed by a capital.

Card tables, with slender legs, now had rectangular folding tops, which could be supported when opened on an extending leg. The top corners were rounded to hold candlesticks. One of the most charming of Queen Anne pieces was the dressing glass, a swing mirror on a shaped stand with tiers of drawers, which stood on the dressing table. Wall mirrors were tall and narrow and had flat frames (Plate 32) shaped at the top, sometimes with a central shell; they were often decorated with gesso (Plate 27).

35. Walnut chair with pierced splat and cabriole legs carved with coquillage; *c.*1735.

36. Walnut chest-on-chest (tallboy) with moulded corners; veneered with burr walnut; *c.*1740.

The Early Mahogany Period: *c.1725-55*

The second quarter of the 18th century produced two major developments—the introduction of mahogany and the entry of the architect into the field of furniture design. Mahogany, the most famous of all furniture woods, was already known in England, but its real introduction to English cabinet-making came towards the end of George I's reign (1714–27), when imports began slowly to increase after the abolition in 1721 of the high duties on West Indian timbers. No finer material could have been put into the hands of the celebrated Georgian craftsmen, whose great skill, stimulated by the demands of the wealthy and cultured upper classes, was to produce the golden age of English cabinet-making.

But mahogany took some time to supersede walnut, which remained in fashion until *c.*1750 (Plate 48). Much walnut furniture of this time has been lost through attack by woodworm. The earliest kind of mahogany was the dark, heavy, straight-grained 'Spanish' wood from San Domingo and Jamaica, which was worked in the solid (Plates 37, 38). At the same time European walnut was largely replaced by Virginia walnut, a dark, unfigured wood also used in the solid. Thus from *c.*1725 to 1750 mahogany and 'black' walnut were both employed by cabinet-makers (Plate 33). Much of this walnut was stained to imitate mahogany.

The fine qualities of mahogany were revealed as more supplies came from Cuba and Honduras. Its metallic strength encouraged experiments in design which had been impossible with other woods, and its great widths made it now unnecessary to join planks for table tops. Soon after 1750 beautifully figured wood was used extensively as a veneer, and could be laid on in larger sheets than had been normal with walnut. In addition, it had a fine patina, a wide range of colour, and resistance to warping and worm.

37. George II card table in San Domingo mahogany, *c.*1745; a good example of the texture and crisp carving of this early 'Spanish' wood.

38. Another example of early mahogany furniture — a gate-leg dining table in 'Spanish' mahogany, with unusual double-octagon top; *c*.1740.

39. Mahogany bureau; *c*.1740.

40. Mahogany armchair upholstered in needlework; legs carved with lion masks and paw feet; c.1740.

41. Mahogany mirror; broken pediment centring in a cartouche; frame carved with Vitruvian scroll; c.1745.

42. Mahogany side table with marble top; carved acanthus and Vitruvian scroll ornament; cabriole legs end on paw feet; *c.*1745.

43. Mahogany stool; legs carved with acanthus leaf and cabochon ornament, and ending on pad feet; *c.*1745.

Mahogany did not greatly affect taste at first. Early mahogany pieces are indistinguishable from their walnut counterparts. But the use of solid wood stimulated carving, hence the 'lion period' from *c.*1725–40 which took its name from the lion's paw feet and lion masks on the knees of cabriole legs (Plate 40), other motives being satyr masks, cabochons and shells, used with claw-and-ball feet. Chair backs began to lose their solid splats and took on an open design of narrow pierced verticals (Plate 35); chair arms often had eagles' head terminals.

Mahogany flap dining tables usually had four or six legs and oval or circular tops, and continued the gate-leg principle by having an extra swing leg on each side to support the flaps (Plate 38). In

44. Mahogany bureau-bookcase with broken pediment; *c.*1740.

45. Walnut and gilt chair; with pierced splat in form of shell, *c.*1745; showing transitional stage between early Georgian and Chippendale styles.

46. Mid-18th-century carved console table with marble top.

some of these tables an extra leaf could be inserted. By 1750 it was usual to build up long dining tables by fastening a semicircular pier table to each end of a centre gate-leg table with two rectangular flaps.

By 1750 also the new fashion for drinking tea greatly increased the demand for the tripod ('pillar and claw') tea table, which had three legs of cabriole form—the claws—dovetailed to the base of a turned pillar (Plate 47). Shortly after that date the top of the tripod table was made to tilt by being hinged to a small cage which was seated on the pillar and wedged to make it fast; the top could be lifted off when the wedge was removed. Square card tables with folding tops were sometimes given a hinged folding ('concertina') framework so that two legs could be extended to hold the flap.

For drawered furniture the cock bead, the most typical of Georgian mouldings, was introduced c.1730 and became universal from c.1745. This projecting moulding was rebated on the edge of the drawer (Fig. 6).

William Kent, 1685–1748. William Kent, artist, architect and landscape-gardener, was the first English architect to include furniture designs in his decorative schemes. Trained as an artist in Italy, and patronised by the cultured Earl of Burlington, he designed the contents of great houses in a monumental baroque style. His furniture—chairs, chests, bookcases, writing tables, pier glasses, 'terms and bustos' (i.e., busts on pedestals), 'marble tables' (i.e., side tables with Italian marble tops) (Plate 42), console tables (introduced from France and supported against the wall by two brackets (Plate 46) or a spread eagle)—was marked by elaborate carved and gilt decoration in softwood, or sometimes in mahogany parcel- (i.e., partly-) gilt. His ornaments included rich swags, human masks and figures, ringed lion heads and, on friezes, the Vitruvian scroll (or wave pattern) (Plates 41, 42) and Greek keys.

Kent's furniture was part of a unified scheme and looks ponderous when removed from its original position. It was conceived in architectural terms and had little influence on cabinet-making in general, though there was a short architectural phase in furniture in which larger cabinets, bookcases, etc., acquired classical architectural elements such as pediments (Plate 44), columns and pilasters, and cabinet-makers were urged to make a thorough study of architectural proportions.

47. Mahogany pillar and claw (tripod) table with finely carved feet and shaft; *c.*1745.

48. Bureau, *c.*1750, veneered with burr walnut—a striking example of the continued fashion for walnut. Made by Elizabeth Bell and Son.

49. Elizabeth Bell's trade label on walnut bureau (Plate 48). Very few Georgian pieces carried their maker's name. Elizabeth Bell continued her late husband's business from *c.*1750 in St Paul's Churchyard, for long the chief centre of furniture-making in London.

Thomas Chippendale (1718-79) and the Rococo Period

Recent research has revealed that among the outstanding cabinet-makers of the early and mid-Georgian periods were the partners John Gumley and James Moore, Benjamin Goodison, William Hallett, William Bradshaw, and the partners, William Vile and John Cobb. Yet the most famous name in popular (and international) estimation remains that of Thomas Chippendale, who has rather unfairly overshadowed his contemporaries, for although his workshop in St Martin's Lane, London, produced elegant furniture for fashionable clients, his was not the finest furniture of this time, and he did not gain a royal appointment. He is famous because in 1754 he launched a new style, the English version of the French rococo, in his pattern book, *A Gentleman and Cabinet-Maker's Director*, the first illustrated catalogue to be published by a cabinet-maker and to be devoted exclusively (in 160 plates) to furniture designs.

The rococo style was a revolt against formal classicism and was marked by a lively use of asymmetrical curves in C and S scrolls, in what Hogarth in 1753 called 'the serpentine line, or line of grace'. Chippendale also incorporated in his book designs for furniture in the Chinese and Gothic tastes, the former inspired by renewed interest in oriental styles, the latter by the Gothic decoration in Horace Walpole's house at Strawberry Hill. Chinese scroll work and figures, and Gothic tracery, blended harmoniously with the rococo, though Chippendale also used Chinese geometrical lattice and fretwork, and some furniture of this period was japanned.

The *Director* was intended to be a guide for craftsmen and wealthy clients. It was re-issued in 1755 and, enlarged to 200 plates, in 1762. Its designs were widely copied and freely adapted, and its success stimulated similar publications by craftsmen and designers. Thus Ince and Mayhew's *Universal System of Household Furniture* (1759–63) was largely based on the *Director*. One cannot,

50. Mahogany armchair; cabriole legs and claw-and-ball feet; splat carved in the rococo taste; *c.*1755.

51. Mahogany armchair, with straight legs and stretchers; splat decorated with Gothic tracery; *c.*1755.

52. Console table finely carved and gilt in the rococo taste; *c.*1755.

53. Mahogany upholstered armchair; arm supports and front legs carved with low relief lattice ornament; pierced stretchers; *c.*1760.

therefore, attribute to Chippendale (as used to be the case) the bulk of surviving furniture of this period in his *Director* style. Only a relatively few pieces can be proved to have come from his workshop, and some of the best of these were made later in his career, when the rococo style was outmoded. The best rococo furniture was made in Vile's workshop.

Characteristic rococo decoration can be seen on chairs (Plate 50), with their serpentine cresting rails, intertwined scrolled splats (sometimes in 'ribband back' form), cabriole legs, and French scroll feet (now replacing the claw-and-ball) (Plate 54); on commodes, the fashionable ornamental chests of drawers which stood prominently in reception rooms and closely followed French models with serpentine fronts and elaborate carvings; on console tables (Plate 52); and on carved and gilt mirror frames, some of which exhibited asymmetrical decoration in its most ornate form. These mirrors often had Chinese pagodas, bells, mandarins, birds, dragons, etc., mingled with scrolled foliage. Gothic motives appeared as arches and pinnacles on chair backs (Plate 51), glazing bars, etc.

The more extravagant *Director* designs do not seem to have been executed, for the traditional English instinct for moderation reasserted itself. Many chairs, for instance, had straight legs on which stretchers were re-introduced (Plate 51).

It was the great strength of mahogany which gave chair backs their daring scrolls and ribbons. The delicacy of the splats was enhanced by chiselling back and narrowing the reverse side of the scrolls, leaving the tool marks visible. Chinese chairs had large-scale lattice work backs (Plate 55) and, in some cases, pierced stretchers; their straight legs, generally square in section, often had a low-relief fret carved on their two outer faces, in the form known as card-cut ornament. The angles between legs and seat frames usually had a fret-cut bracket, the frames themselves sometimes having a strip of mahogany glued on, card-cut or pierced.

Library furniture received much attention in the *Director*. Since *c.*1745 the break-front bookcase (i.e., with projecting centre section) had come into use and continued to have architectural form with triangular or broken pediments. Open pedestal library tables were favoured, but no designs for

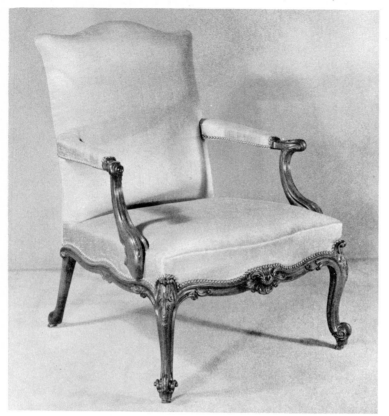

54. Mahogany armchair of the type described in Chippendale's *Director* as 'French'; *c*.1760.

55. Mahogany armchair; back filled with lattice work in the Chinese taste; *c*.1760

56. Mirror with carved and gilt foliage ornament;
c.1755.

57. Chippendale period carved mahogany three-tier
dumb waiter; c.1760.

58. Mahogany tea (or 'china') table; gallery pierced with lattice work in the Chinese taste; low relief carving on legs; pierced stretchers; *c*.1760.

dining tables were given, as these were still made up of separate units and were apparently of little interest to the designer. On the other hand, there were varied designs for writing, breakfast and tea (or 'china') tables (Plate 58). About 1760 the best pillar and claw tables had either a circular top bordered by a gallery or carved ornament, or a scalloped and raised ('piecrust') edge.

Bureau-bookcases had various elaborate designs and were intended to have glazed doors—a reversion to the tradition of the early part of the century. They were surmounted by a crested arch, swan-neck pediment or pierced fret gallery. China cabinets were appropriately given Chinese decoration, with a pierced frieze or pagoda roof.

59. Mahogany serpentine-fronted writing table with pull-out front section; scrolled brackets between legs and top; *c*.1760.

60. Mahogany serpentine-fronted chest of drawers; fluted and reeded canted corners.

61. An example of English devotion to French styles; an unusually early English version of a French *bonheur-du-jour*, with key pattern decoration; *c.*1760.

The Neo-Classical Period

Robert Adam (1728–92). In the 1760's the Chippendale style was replaced by Robert Adam's classical revival. Adam, the most famous of the Georgian architect-designers, was of Scottish origin and the second of four brothers who established an architectural firm in London shortly after 1758. Inspired by his studies of classical and Renaissance architecture in Dalmatia and Italy between 1754 and 1758, he developed the neo-classical style, a graceful and delicate version of classical forms and decoration. English furniture was to be immensely influenced by what Sir John Soane in 1812 called 'the electric power of this Revolution in Art'.

Some of Adam's furniture designs, which were 'invented for particular persons', were published in *The Works of Robert and James Adam*, the first part of which appeared in 1773. They were translated into practical, everyday furniture by George Hepplewhite's *Cabinet-Maker and Upholsterer's Guide* of 1788, a pattern book which showed the type of furniture generally made between 1775 and 1800.

Like Kent, but in much more detail, Adam planned the whole of the interior decoration and furnishing of his houses to conform to a unified pattern. Among his characteristic decorative motives were festoons of husks (Plate 69), vases, honeysuckle, paterae, rams' and satyrs' heads, and medallions, applied in a variety of ways—by painting, carving, fine inlay or in ormolu. Painting was usually carried out directly on beech, but it was also done on harewood and satinwood veneers in the form of festoons, borders and medallions, and sometimes copper panels or suitably shaped pieces of paper (Plates 70, 71) were first painted and then inserted into or glued on the furniture. Fine inlay is the name given to the marquetry of classical decoration now revived by Adam, to distinguish it from the marquetry of the Stuart period; the techniques of cutting and application were the same. By 1800 painted furniture had become so popular that it had largely superseded marquetry.

62. Mahogany serpentine card table; *c*.1765.

63. Large gilt settee in the French taste; *c.*1770.

64. Mahogany Pembroke table, with serpentine ends to flaps; fluted and tapered legs; inlaid paterae above legs; *c.*1770.

65. Mahogany armchair of *bergère* type with caned back; decorated with carved fluting and paterae; *c* 1775.

66. Mahogany bureau, with inlaid decoration on flap in form of ribbon; *c*.1770.

67. Mahogany 'spider leg' gate-leg table with slender turned legs; *c*.1765.

68. Serpentine-fronted commode decorated with marquetry in the French taste; *c*.1780.

69. Chair in neo-classical taste; carved husk decoration of back centres in honeysuckle on middle rib of splat; c.1775.

70. Triangular corner table, carved and gilded; with painted decoration on frieze, top and stretcher platform in neo-classical taste.

71. *Above:* The delicacy of Adam period decoration is well illustrated in this detail of the top of the table in plate 70, painted in black and white on paper.

72. Mahogany armchair of *c.*1775 based on French models—a concession to the influence exercised by France on the English upper classes.

73. Satinwood bureau-bookcase of *c*.1780, decorated with carved frieze, inlay and painted panels; drawer front in lower stage lets down to form writing top; cupboard door lets down to disclose four central drawers flanked by recesses for books; oval panels in upper stage filled with patterned material.

74. Mahogany shield-back chair of type always associated with Hepplewhite; carved wheat-ears and rosette on back; fluted legs.

75. Window seat painted with floral sprays and medallions, *c*.1790. Painted and japanned decoration was popularised by Robert Adam and Hepplewhite.

Bright ormolu mounts of classical design were used to great effect on a dark mahogany background. Ormolu is the term for fire-gilt bronze and brass; the metal, after chasing, was first coated with an amalgam of gold and mercury, then fired at a high temperature. This caused the mercury to evaporate and the gold to adhere to the metal, which could be brightly burnished. Ormolu mounts, formerly imported from France, were made for the first time in England by Matthew Boulton from 1762.

French influence is apparent in Adam's upholstered chairs, which had oval backs (Plate 72) and taper-turned or serpentine front legs, the latter ending on scroll feet. His neo-classical chairs had round or oval (Plate 69) or rectilinear (some lyre-shaped) backs; their legs were usually of square tapering form and decorated with fluting which ended above a solid plinth; oval or circular paterae were often carved on the level of the seat rail. Small semicircular side tables, commodes, cabinets, mirrors and stands were other favourite pieces for classical decoration. A novel combination of a side table and two flanking pedestal cupboards, each surmounted by an urn, was the precursor of the modern sideboard.

After *c*.1765 the attractive Pembroke table (Plates 64, 86, 88) in mahogany or satinwood became fashionable. It had obvious links with the older double flap gate-leg table, and had an oval or rectangular top; the central (fixed) portion was larger than that of the earlier tables as the two flaps were now supported by wooden (usually beech) brackets attached by wooden hinges to the framework.

Much of Adam's furniture was decorated with veneers of West Indian and Guiana satinwood (Plate 73), of which the light yellow tone enhanced the delicacy of his designs, especially against the pastel shades which he favoured for the walls of his rooms. The last part of the century is sometimes called 'the age of satinwood'. Adam's clients contracted with several leading cabinet-makers to execute his designs; among them was Chippendale, whose finest authenticated pieces were made for Adam's houses.

76. Mahogany armchair, centre splat headed by three plumes. The number of designs of chairs with square backs was increased in the third edition (1794) of Hepplewhite's *Guide* to compete with Sheraton's *Drawing Book* (1791–4).

77. Mahogany serpentine-fronted sideboard with fluted legs and carved paterae on the frieze; *c*.1780.

George Hepplewhite (d.1786). As stated in its preface, Hepplewhite's *Guide*, with some 300 plates, 'designedly followed the latest or most prevailing fashion only', thus avowing its aim of popularising Adam's neo-classical style. Although it was an important and successful book (second edition, 1789; third edition, revised, 1794), very little is known about Hepplewhite himself. After apprenticeship to Gillow of Lancaster, he came to London and had a business in Cripplegate, but no furniture from his workshop has ever been identified. The *Guide* was published by his widow two years after his death, and it has never been determined how many of the designs were Hepplewhite's own or were those of collaborators.

Nevertheless, the *Guide* is a landmark in English furniture history for its skilful adaptation of Adam's designs into light and elegant furniture, free from exaggerated ornament, and intended to be made in mahogany and satinwood, or painted (Plate 75) or japanned. The many surviving graceful pieces of his period illustrate the fine standard of English craftsmanship and the excellent quality of the woods used.

The most famous of Hepplewhite's chair designs is the shield-back, which he developed but did not originate (Plate 74). He also used oval and heart shapes. Most of these chair backs did not have the splat connected with the seat but were supported as a framework by the upward prolongation of the back legs. Their decoration was carved or, if they were intended for drawing-rooms and bedrooms, painted or japanned. On carved chairs the frame was channelled (i.e., slightly sunk) and embellished with motives in neo-classical taste—vases, honeysuckle, festoons of husks, etc., and also draperies, wheatears and foliage. A novelty was the Prince of Wales's feathers, which Hepplewhite may have invented.

Usually chair legs were of square section, tapering slightly to plinth feet. The supports for chair arms now swept back from just above the front legs and up to the arms, which joined the back about half way up. In contrast, Hepplewhite also designed backs of square form, filled with rows of vertical bars (Plate 76).

78. Mahogany library table decorated with enamel plaques on the drawers; this table resembles a type illustrated in Hepplewhite's *Guide; c.*1785.

79. Mahogany cabinet; upper stage has inlaid floral decoration and Gothic glazing bars; c.1780.

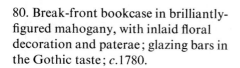

80. Break-front bookcase in brilliantly-figured mahogany, with inlaid floral decoration and paterae; glazing bars in the Gothic taste; c.1780.

Towards the end of the century chests of drawers tended to become taller, often with a wide frieze above the top drawer. Sheraton illustrated two (which he called 'dressing chests') with a shallow drawer fitted for writing. The front corners were finished with reeded pilasters, square or round, ending on short turned feet.

It is no exaggeration to consider the Sheraton period as marking the height of technical accomplishment in English cabinet-making, for delicacy, strength and utility are found combined to a greater degree in furniture then than at any other time.

87. Oval mahogany folding dining table with inlaid decoration; c.1785.

88. Pembroke table with rectangular flaps, decorated with veneers of burr yew and inlaid 'stringing'; c.1785.

Regency Furniture: c.1800-30

When applied to English furniture, the term 'Regency' covers a wider period than the political Regency of 1811–20. It is a descriptive label for the revived classicism which sprang from the archaeological study of antiquities, and aimed at copying or adapting to modern usage the furniture of ancient Egypt, Greece and Rome. This fashion for classical purity, already evident in France, was introduced into England by the architect, Henry Holland (d.1806). His refurnishing of Carlton House (from 1783) for the Prince of Wales showed strong French influences; and at Southill (from 1796) the furniture made under his direction or from his designs incorporated both the late Louis XVI style and the new classical details (which were based on drawings sent to him from Rome by his pupil, C. H. Tatham). The strictly archaeological approach to furniture was at first confined to leaders of taste, and in England was interpreted in a scholarly way by Thomas Hope in his *Household Furniture and Interior Decoration* (1807), a collection of drawings which the author, a wealthy and widely-travelled connoisseur, used as designs for the furniture of his London home. Some evidence of this new approach appeared in Sheraton's later works, but when it was taken up fully by cabinet-makers, as in George Smith's *A Collection of Designs for Household Furniture* (1808), it tended to become an incongruous mixture of styles.

The best Regency furniture, however, showed admirable proportions and fine craftsmanship. Emphasis was laid on unbroken surfaces and straight lines, for contemporary opinion considered that ancient furniture was 'almost universally distinguished by straight or angular lines'. Dark, glossy woods with striped figures were used to set off the bright brass (Plates 96, 99) now widely employed for inlay, trellis work, galleries, lion paw feet, lion mask handles, star-shaped bolt heads, and studs. Rosewood from Brazil was in great favour (Plates 96, 98); so too were suitable selections of mahogany,

89. Early 19th-century serpentine-fronted occasional table with semicircular ends; inlaid decoration on top.

90. Early 19th-century bureau with cylindrical top, veneered with amboyna wood.

91. Mahogany folding-top table with sphinx heads, legs of animal form and decoration in the Egyptian taste; *c.*1805.

92. *Left:* Armchair in the Egyptian taste, *c*.1805. The cross-framed front legs are typical of the Regency period. 93. *Right:* Regency mahogany armchair of classical form, with wide shoulder board, key pattern decoration on the cross-rail and 'sabre' front legs; *c*.1805.

calamander and zebra-wood. Many pieces of furniture were of low height (Plate 96), their angular lines accentuated by reeding, so that the wall above them could have plenty of space for pictures.

Graeco-Roman ornament was faithfully reproduced with a new precision, particularly the palmette and anthemion (i.e., conventionalised honeysuckle design). A special feature was the use of Egyptian motives inspired by Napoleon's expedition to Egypt in 1798 and by the report of his chief archaeologist, Denon, in 1802. In England, Nelson's victory at the Nile (1798) made the Egyptian revival a fashionable craze (Plates 91, 92), of which the chief popular symbols were Egyptian heads and feet, the lotus flower and bud, hieroglyphics, griffons, serpents and crocodiles.

'Grecian' chairs became fashionable, characterised by bold, simple outlines, wide shoulder boards and 'sabre' front legs (Plate 93), these last two features being often also found on other chairs of the time. Also popular was the sofa or couch, in either the classical form of curved head-end and short arm-rests, or with a continuous padded back joining two curved ends.

Two new types of table are particularly associated with the Regency period—the circular-top table on a pillar and claw or pedestal base; and the sofa table (Plates 99, 100), which developed from, though it did not supersede, the Pembroke table, and had a rectangular top with two end flaps. These sofa tables had either two trestle-type ends connected by a stretcher, or were supported by columns or a pedestal on a platform with outward curving feet. Smaller tables included 'quartetto' tables, or nests of four, ladies' work tables with pouches for sewing materials, and tables for writing, reading, games, etc. There was a return to fashion of longer dining tables of extending type, with pillar and claw supports (Plate 94); large round ones, however, were also made.

The lighter type of sideboard of the Hepplewhite and Sheraton periods gave way to the revived table and pedestal cupboards which Adam had introduced, or to a large side table with a brass gallery on top and a wine cooler beneath. In contrast, there were a number of small bookcases with glazed or wire trellis doors backed by material, and chiffoniers, low cupboards with book shelves. A well-known Regency piece was the convex mirror enclosed by a circular, hollow-moulded frame.

The Victorian Period: 1837-1901

Victorian furniture has often been criticised, with much justification, for its poor design and ornate decoration. Rapid industrialisation and the great increase in the population led to a vast output of cheap furniture which, though it was not itself made by machinery to any appreciable extent until the end of Victoria's reign, was certainly influenced by the debased standard of many other machine-made articles, and was often characterised by hurried workmanship and shoddy materials. Even the best furniture, of good craftsmanship and materials, was often tastelessly elaborate. But recent research has led to considerable re-appraisal of Victorian furniture design. In particular, it is now recognised that the very ornate furniture at the Great Exhibition of 1851 was by no means typical, as many writers have supposed, of the period, but was, on the contrary, freely criticised by contemporaries for its showiness (Plate 101).

Moreover, much competent and interesting work was done by designers and architects (who increasingly turned their attention to furniture design), and by the end of the reign, under the inspiration of William Morris, there was a marked revival of good craftsmanship. Unfortunately, the work of these designers was too often debased by indiscriminate imitations by commercial firms who sought to catch the prevailing fashion without really understanding it.

Two important factors influenced Victorian furniture. One was the stress on comfort, for social life centred in the home and family. The rising standard of living and the rapid growth of cities gave more people than ever before the chance to rent or buy and furnish a home of their own. Cheap factory-produced textiles covered seat furniture with deep upholstery and tables with thick draperies so that the elegant framework of such furniture was lost. The second factor was the revival of historical styles, among which the Gothic predominated; this marked the end of classical supremacy and cleared the way for experimentation.

101. Design for a walnut and ebony carved cabinet by Freeman of Norwich, sent to the Great Exhibition of 1851.

102. Chair with upholstered seat and back panel, made of walnut. A style often described by Victorians as 'Elizabethan'.

103. Early Victorian sofa at Sheringham Hall, Norfolk. The deep buttoning so popular at this date can be seen here.

104. *Left:* Victorian mahogany balloon-back chair with upholstered seat, made by G. M. & H. J. Story of London Wall. 105. *Right:* 'Prie-dieu' or kneeling chair. Chairs of this design were popular throughout the early and mid-Victorian periods.

Early Victorian, 1837–60. In the thirty years after 1830 the standard of furniture design was particularly poor. Loudon's *Encyclopaedia* (1833)— its re-issue, practically unaltered, in several subsequent editions showed how much furniture lacked original ideas—named four prevailing styles: the Grecian (i.e., classical), Gothic, Elizabethan, and Louis XIV. But as art history was then in its infancy, the exact interpretation of these styles was by no means clear. Thus the Gothic and Elizabethan, both considered sturdy national styles, were frequently confused, and much 'Elizabethan' furniture was really reproduction of (often late) Stuart pieces (Plate 102). The Louis XIV or 'old French style' incorporated much of the Louis XV period and was inspired by the revival of *ancien régime* furniture in France after the Bourbon restoration of 1815.

Padded upholstery, which comfortably clothed chairs, sofas (Plate 103) and ottomans, influenced other types of furniture, for straight lines and rectangular shapes were abandoned for curves, rounded corners and semicircular plans. Wherever possible, surfaces were left plain and French polished, for inlay was out of fashion. Sideboards acquired mirror backboards, often three in number, with semicircular crests.

In spite of the confusion, this period produced two original chair designs. One was the balloon-back, which derived from both the Grecian chair with its broad shoulder board, and the scrolled Louis XIV type, until, between 1835 and 1850, the rail and uprights formed a continuous curve pinched at the waist by a cross-rail (Plate 104). The other was the 'prie-dieu', with a tall upholstered back and low seat and legs, which was clearly based on Charles II chairs but was at that time considered typically Tudor (Plate 105).

106. Early Victorian papier-mâché circular or loo table.

107. The Kenilworth Sideboard or Buffet (Warwick Castle), made by Cookes of Warwick, is one of the best known pieces produced by the Warwickshire carvers.

108. Oak table designed by Philip Webb; c.1870. Webb was the chief designer for William Morris's firm.

The early Victorians were fond of experimenting with a variety of materials besides wood for furniture. Some, like Derbyshire marble, had only limited success, but much furniture was made of metal, such as cast-iron chairs, benches and hall furniture, and iron and brass bedsteads, which were considered more hygienic than wooden ones and rapidly supplanted them. Italian marble was also widely used in bedrooms for washstand tops.

But the most popular of these materials today is papier-mâché, which was known in the 18th century and used for furniture from the 1820's. It was made in two ways, either by pasting sheets of paper on moulds, or by pressing paper pulp between dies. The result was a smooth, hard surface which was usually painted with floral decoration on a shining black background, or inlaid with mother-of-pearl (Plate 106). The amount of this furniture produced, however, has been exaggerated. Most of it was made by one firm, Jennens and Bettridge of Birmingham, and the papier-mâché was normally combined on furniture with structural members of wood or metal.

This period saw a revival of woodcarving, which was a dying craft during the Regency. A feature of some of the more elaborate pieces was their 'anecdotal' carving of scenes from popular romances and poems, or from local history or, on sideboards, of fruit and emblems of the chase. There were prominent schools of woodcarving in London, Tyneside and Warwick (Plate 107). Amateur enthusiasm was encouraged for the craft, aided by fret-carving machines in the home, and this, with the coming of machine carving, explains the mass of pseudo-medieval and Renaissance carving on much late Victorian furniture.

Late Victorian, 1860–1901.   (a) WILLIAM MORRIS. Appalled by the ugliness of commercially-made articles, William Morris with some friends founded in 1861 the firm of Morris & Co. with the aim of making, by hand, artistic objects for home use, in accordance with his famous dictum, 'Have nothing in your house that you do not know to be useful or believe to be beautiful'. Morris himself does not seem to have designed furniture, but his firm employed, among others, the artist Ford Madox Brown and the architect Philip Webb to design simple workaday furniture, mainly in oak (Plate 108).

109. Wardrobe designed by Philip Webb, as a wedding present for William Morris. Door panels painted by Edward Burne-Jones in 1858.

110. Escritoire and stand made by Morris & Co. in 1893 and designed by George Jack. The marquetry is of sycamore and other woods.

111. Oak sideboard with carved boxwood panels and metal hinges, designed by Bruce Talbert and exhibited in the London Exhibition of 1873.

112. Dining room sideboard illustrated in *Hints on Household Taste*, by Charles L. Eastlake (1868).

In particular, the firm produced two famous chairs; one, which sold for five shillings, had turned ebonised beech frame and supports, and a rush seat adapted from a traditional Sussex country type; the other was an upholstered, adjustable arm-chair which attained great popularity in America as well as Britain. More ornamental 'state-furniture' was also made, mainly designed by Webb and painted by Morris, his friend Burne-Jones, and other artists of the Pre-Raphaelite school (Plate 109).

All this work was inspired by Morris's enthusiasm for the medieval period which he believed was unsurpassed for the skill of its craftsmen and their honesty of purpose. But c.1890 the character of the firm's furniture, though still of the highest quality, changed under the direction of the architect George Jack, who used mahogany and rosewood decorated with elaborate marquetry in the 18th century tradition (Plate 110), and of W. A. S. Benson, who incorporated a great deal of metalwork into his furniture.

Many of the firm's products proved too expensive for most homes, but Morris's ideals, forcefully expressed through his writings and speeches, were a powerful factor in checking the decay in standards of taste.

(b) ART FURNITURE. The period from the 1860's to the 1880's saw the 'art furniture' movement, a phrase loosely used to denote an emphasis on historical (mainly Gothic) styles. In spite of its abuse by manufacturers, this movement had much of interest and indeed of originality. It was launched by the publication of two designers, Bruce Talbert's *Gothic Forms Applied to Furniture* (1867) (Plate 111), and C. L. Eastlake's *Hints on Household Taste* (1868) (Plate 112). Their furniture aimed at a more practical Gothic style, emphasising rectangular lines and avoiding curves and ornate carving. Painting replaced carving as their accepted form of decoration.

The architect William Burges designed some highly original Gothic pieces based on his researches into medieval furniture, which he believed was all of simple sturdy form, covered with paintings (Plate 113). Burges was also one of the first to use Japanese motives, which were considered to reflect the same ideals as those of medieval England. But the chief interpreter of this Anglo-Japanese style, popular in the 1870's and 1880's, aided by the interest created by the opening-up of Japan by the West, was another architect, E. W. Godwin, who designed light and delicate furniture with slender supports which set a fashion in ebonised woods and forecast a return to simple, graceful lines (Plate 114).

113. Wash-stand designed by William Burges (1827–81) for his house in Melbury Road, London.

114. Coffee table and chair, both made of
ebonised oak, designed by E. W. Godwin (1833–86).

115. Cabinet made in 1871 by Collinson and
Locke, designed by T. E. Collcutt and made of
ebonised mahogany with painted decoration.

116. Oak sideboard designed by W. R.
Lethaby, c.1900. The piece is lightly carved and
inlaid with ebony, sycamore and bleached
mahogany.

117. Oak cabinet, painted in red and gold,
designed by C. R. Ashbee and made by the Guild
of Handicraft in 1889.

118. Oak desk with brass hinges designed by C.F. Voysey and made by W. H. Tingey in 1896.

Yet another prominent architect, T. E. Collcutt, designed a whole range of furniture for leading firms, from simple oak in the Webb spirit to detailed marquetry far removed from the medieval (Plate 115). He was particularly successful with dining-room chairs with two rows of small turned balusters on the back, above and below a central leather panel.

(c) THE ARTS AND CRAFTS MOVEMENT. Morris's influence was potently marked in the last twenty years of Victoria's reign in the Arts and Crafts Movement, which sprang from the formation of various guilds and societies of craftsmen and designers, mainly directed by architects, to combine social reform with the revival of good design and skilled, honest craftsmanship. The pioneer was the Century Guild of 1882 founded by A. H. Mackmurdo, followed by the Art Workers' Guild (1884), and the Arts and Crafts Exhibition Society and C. R. Ashbee's Guild and School of Handicraft (both 1888).

These societies spread their ideas through numerous exhibitions. Their furniture was by no means confined to the austere cottage-style joinery of the early Morris type, but, on the contrary, showed increasing interest in the 18th century (as evidenced by Morris & Co.'s later pieces) and moreover sometimes incorporated into furniture the work of other craftsmen (in stained glass, ivory, brass, etc.) (Plates 116, 117).

But Morris's ideas were most faithfully carried out, in design, techniques and workshop organisation, by the Cotswold School. This was an offshoot of the short-lived Kenton & Co. (1890–92), another Arts and Crafts Society formed by a group of architects, whose aim was to produce pieces of furniture each one of which was made entirely by one craftsman. Directly inspired by Morris, three members, Ernest Gimson and Sidney and Ernest Barnsley, set up a workshop near Cirencester in the Cotswolds in 1893. Gimson had already mastered the technique of chair-making through instruction from a Herefordshire chair-maker; now he concentrated on design, in close co-operation with his craftsmen. The result was the production of well-designed, beautifully-made and elegant furniture which, by keeping alive the best traditions of English rural craftsmanship, did more than anything else, as far as furniture is concerned, to hand Morris's ideas down to the 20th century.

119. Oak armchair and table, designed by Charles Rennie Mackintosh, *c.*1900.

(d) ART NOUVEAU. *Art Nouveau* was a short-lived, much-discussed but in many ways interesting phase which occurred at the end of Victoria's reign. As in many other instances, the style was so abused by the trade that though its inception owed much to English designers, by 1900 it was regarded as vulgar and foreign, and termed the 'Quaint Style'.

It began as a deliberate attempt to seek a new style for the 20th century. Among its general features were the continuation of the legs of chairs, tables, beds, sideboards, desks, etc., upwards, to end as free-standing columns with flat caps or, more rarely, under a moulding or cornice; a great deal of inlay in various materials, including stained glass; fretwork hearts and machine-made repoussé copper tulips (a favourite emblem of the style); the placing of stretchers on chairs and tables at just above floor level; and the incorporation of archaically-worded mottoes.

Some furniture of outstandingly individual character was designed, however, from 1893 by the architect, C. F. Voysey, who was regarded abroad as the fountainhead of *Art Nouveau* (Plate 118). Like the Arts and Crafts designers he used unstained and unpolished oak, but his own contributions were upward-continuing legs emphasising vertical lines, large door hinges ending in flat hearts, and chairs with thin, elegant uprights. Voysey's furniture was made mainly for individual clients in specially designed interiors which in their simplicity marked the first real break from the crowded and over-decorated Victorian rooms.

Some highly original furniture was also designed by the Glasgow architect, C. R. Mackintosh, particularly high-backed chairs, some as much as five feet tall. At that time, however, his furniture met with little appreciation in England, in spite of its welcome abroad as well as in Scotland, where it fitted admirably into its specially designed interiors (Plate 119).

The Twentieth Century

Up to 1920. The present century has seen the coming of the 'Modern Movement', which has slowly swept away Victorian historicism and done much to restore honesty and fitness of purpose to furniture design. It has meant an innovation of immense importance—the advent of the industrial designer, trained, with full awareness of the character of modern materials and methods, to design furniture of quality for large-scale production by machinery. This marks a technical revolution in furniture-making as far-reaching in its consequences as that of the panel and frame construction in the oak period, and of veneering in the walnut period.

Like these two great changes of the 15th and 17th centuries, machine art has reached England from abroad, this time from Germany and Scandinavia. It has by no means replaced hand craft, which has strongly maintained the traditions established by Gimson, who died in 1919. Thus the craftsman who produces single pieces, and the machine which makes a large number (with all the advantages of rapidity and cheapness) make up a complementary process of great value in the development of furniture, as long as the design and quality resulting from both methods are first rate. But the struggle to escape from the worst influences of the Victorian era and to establish sound principles of design, and above all to educate public taste to a proper understanding of machine art, has been long and difficult.

Until 1914 the exhibitions of the various members of the Arts and Crafts Movement continued to display furniture which illustrated the basic features of Morris's message—a thorough knowledge of materials and the setting and maintenance of the highest possible standard of craftsmanship in every detail. This furniture, and particularly that of Gimson, was among the most interesting then being made in Europe, and indeed received more attention abroad than at home, where it was appreciated by only a minority, most people being preoccupied with reproductions and the last phase of *Art Nouveau*.

120. Oak wardrobe designed by Ambrose Heal *c.*1900. Exhibited at Paris Exhibition. Inlaid with ivory and mother-of-pearl.

121. Chestnut wardrobe with one long drawer and interior all hanging space. Designed by Ambrose Heal, 1912.

122. Cherry wood and walnut bookcase. Designed by Ambrose Heal; c.1915.

123. Cabinet of English walnut with ebony glazing bars and edgings; *c.*1922 (Heal).

124. Weathered oak bureau designed by Ambrose Heal; *c.*1928.

125. Nursery dresser by Ambrose Heal, 1935.

The great mistake in Morris's teaching was his refusal to consider using machinery to make cheap and well-designed objects for everyday use. It was in Germany that the wider implications of his doctrine—that the ordinary man's house should be filled with pleasant things—were recognised in the foundation, in 1907, of the Werkbund, a group of architects, artists and manufacturers whose intention was to produce objects of high quality by machine as well as by hand; for, as was said at the inaugural address, 'it is not the machines in themselves that make work inferior, but our inability to use them properly'. The next stage in Germany was the establishment of the famous Bauhaus under Walter Gropius in 1919 to train 'furniture architects' to design for the machine, and this rapidly became the main centre of creative design in Europe.

In England the pioneer of commercially-produced furniture of good progressive design was Ambrose Heal (1872–1959), whose work in this field at this time ranks in value with Gimson's achievements in hand craft. Heal was reared in the Arts and Crafts Movement, whose principles he now carried into the furniture trade. Indicative of the new trends was the wardrobe he exhibited at the Paris Exhibition of 1900, with its plain surfaces of fumed and waxed oak and small inlaid panels of ivory and mother-of-pearl (Plate 120). But even more important than fine exhibition pieces has been the production by Heal's firm of simple pieces of good lines and fine materials for the ordinary market (Plates 121–125). As early as 1898 the firm's first catalogue of Plain Oak Furniture began the revival of simple wooden bedsteads of pleasant design which were to become very popular in the trade.

From 1920 to 1945. The lack in England of real experience of designing good furniture for machine production was clearly illustrated after the First World War. The immense building and furnishing boom of the 1920's encouraged the rapid output of furniture and almost complete use of mechanised processes. The design of this commercial furniture was, however, usually as poor as the materials

126. Fall-front writing cabinet in English oak with solid burr oak panels. Designed by Gordon Russell, 1921.

127. Chair in English oak; leather seat. Designed by Gordon Russell, 1924.

128. Sideboard in English oak, with yew and ebony handles. Designed by Gordon Russell, 1924, and exhibited at Paris Exhibition.

129. Dressing table and chair in Australian walnut designed by Gordon Russell in 1928 to be made largely by machine.

130. Desk in walnut with black cellulosed top and veneered ply end panels. Designed by Gordon Russell, 1934, for machine production.

with which it was made. The curious revival of pseudo-historical styles—Elizabethan, Jacobean, late Stuart, etc.—inspired such absurdities as the application of machine-made 'bulbs', carvings and mouldings to carcases, and it is possible that future generations will regard the furniture of these years as among the worst ever made in England. For 'traditional' was regarded merely as a spur to imitate the past, and not to design furniture in a straightforward way, with proper understanding of new materials and methods (as the great designers of the past had done).

Yet progress towards good design and craftsmanship has continued. Gordon Russell (b.1892) has provided the link between Gimson on the one hand and the continental 'furniture-architects' on the other (Plates 126–131). It is significant that he began his career as a designer at Broadway, Worcestershire, at about the time of Gimson's death, in the Arts and Crafts tradition, but has moved to designing also for machine production (Plates 129, 130). An important year was 1929, when the first of his radio cabinets for factory production showed a complete understanding of the nature of the problem and a triumphant solution. To have put a radio set in a 'reproduction' case would have been in the worst possible taste; instead, the advance now achieved in design, as successful as in the cases made by craftsmen (who faced a very similar problem) for the clocks of the late Stuart era, gave the best English radio cabinets a higher standard of design than anywhere else in the world.

The original Russell workshop at Broadway and the factory which has grown up behind it symbolise the joint triumph of hand and machine craft. Public interest was also aroused in the remarkable progress abroad in machine work, particularly in Scandinavia, where the Finnish architect, Alvar Aalto, designed some admirable furniture.

Meanwhile, at Petersfield, Hampshire, Edward Barnsley (b.1900), the son of Sidney Barnsley, Gimson's collaborator, established a small workshop on the Gimson model and produced furniture which clearly demonstrated that the finest traditions of the past were being fully maintained (Plates 132–135). An increasing number of small shops, including that of Peter Waals, formerly Gimson's foreman, and also the workshops at Heal's and Russell's, made similar furniture of high quality by hand.

131. Circular table and chairs
designed by W. H. Russell, 1950.

132. Bow-fronted chest of drawers in
figured black bean inlaid with holly.
Edward Barnsley, 1956.

The Second World War saw a unique experiment, the introduction of 'utility' furniture of standard specifications and designs necessitated by the shortage of timber and the loss of furniture through enemy action. A committee of eminent designers appointed by the Board of Trade drew up designs for the whole range of furniture, which were much better and simpler than had been common in the pre-war years. Although permanent control of this kind would hardly be desirable, and although the scheme did not perhaps meet the immediate success in the post-war years which its sponsors had hoped for (for many manufacturers reverted to period elaboration in their furniture, explaining that the public found 'utility' designs too plain), yet there is little doubt that the good proportions and clean lines of the well-designed furniture of the war period has had its effect.

The Post-War Scene. This increased interest in good furniture is very evident today. Hand craftsmanship of high order flourishes among a number of workshops throughout the country (Plate 136), of which Edward Barnsley's is still the best known. Their work is encouraged by such bodies as the Craft Centre and the Rural Industries Bureau. Craft work, taught by well-qualified teachers, is firmly established in the schools. A decided stimulus to the appreciation of machine work has come from the Council of Industrial Design and its permanent display at the Design Centre in London. A clear symptom of this interest has been the close attention paid in the post-war years to Danish factory-made furniture, which has achieved a great reputation for its skilful and attractive design.

Modern industry has produced machines for all the furniture-making processes, and materials for constructing furniture, which are quite different from the traditional ones. Woodworking machines have, in fact, a long history behind them, for in 1793 Sir Samuel Bentham took out an inclusive patent for machines for planing, sawing, moulding, etc. for large-scale work, and carving machines

133. China cabinet of rosewood inlaid with holly, Edward Barnsley, 1958.

134. Dressing table in Indian rosewood inlaid with holly. Edward Barnsley, 1961.

135. Small sideboard in black bean, with tambour doors. Edward Barnsley.

136. Sideboard in solid English yew, with sliding tambour doors. Alan Peters.

were in use before the Great Exhibition, but these were very different from the precision furniture-making machines which are in use today. Veneers can be cut rapidly and cheaply by machine, either by peeling with a rotary cutter, which feeds a long knife into a revolving log after it has been steamed, or by slicing with a knife, in which case the logs are first sawn into flitches and then cut horizontally by the knife moving across the flitch or vertically by the knife moving nearer the flitch after each stroke.

Modern man-made timber materials have remarkable properties. Plywood is built up of uneven numbers of veneers glued together so that the grain of any ply is at right angles to that of adjacent plies. Blockboard consists of a core of wood strips about an inch wide sandwiched between veneers with their grain at right angles to that of the core. Laminboard is similar except that it has a core of thinner strips. Chipboard is composed of wood chips bonded under pressure with resin glues. All these materials have the great advantage over solid wood in that they do not split or warp; they are light and strong, ideal for large, unbroken surfaces, and can be veneered with selected timbers. Plywood in particular has immense strength, and can moreover be bent to curved shapes without damage, and even joined to metals by glues. One sheet of bent plywood can form the sides and bottom of a drawer, which is thus light and easy to clean.

Methods of steaming and bending timber also have a long history, for they were used by Michael Thonet in Germany in the 1830's. Recent developments in this line have produced structural members of great strength combined with lightness. It is possible, for example, to bend a single piece of prepared wood to form three sides of a rectangle and thus make the arm, front leg and support of each side of a chair, without the need of a back leg.

For jointing, machine-made dovetails are cut with revolving cutters which form both dovetails and pins in one operation on the two members to be jointed. Such dovetails show equal spacing of pin and dovetail, in contrast to hand-made joints, in which the pin is smaller than the dovetail. Very strong adhesives have been developed as a result of the use of plywoods, so that it is now possible to glue structural members together, such as a stretcher to a leg, without any other form of joint at all. Other types of fittings, developed from the modern use of metals, plastics and nylon, entirely eliminate the need for gluing, jointing and screwing, and are most useful for assembling unit furniture. There are constant improvements in plastics, and in cellulose finishes. All these materials are used by, and indeed serve to stimulate, competent designers.

Appendix I

GLOSSARY OF TECHNICAL AND DECORATIVE TERMS

Acanthus. Conventionalised leaf of classical architecture; much used as carved decoration on 17th- and especially 18th-century furniture (Plates 37, 43, 45).

Amorini. Cupids carved on Charles II chairs and other furniture after 1660 (Plate 22).

Anthemion. Ornament related to honeysuckle; more strictly, frieze with alternating honeysuckle and palmette (*q.v.*). Much used in Adam period, and with classical precision during Regency (Plates 69, 71).

Apron Piece. Ornamental rail connecting tops of legs on chairs and tables, and bracket feet on chests of drawers, etc. (Plates 40, 42).

Arabesque. Ornament of interwoven foliage, scroll work, geometric patterns, etc. (fanciful version of Islamic designs) used in 'seaweed' marquetry from *c.*1690, on gesso tables, *c.*1690–1730, and to some extent after 1760 (Plate 29).

Arcading. Series of arches on pillars carved on panels, especially in early 17th-century work (Plate 12).

Astragal. Small semicircular moulding often placed at junction of doors to keep out dust; or loosely descriptive of glazing bars of later Georgian period.

Back Stool. Chair without arms, as termed in 17th century.

Ball Foot. Spherical base of turned leg mainly in use in late 17th century (Plates 18, 25).

Baluster. Turned column, straight, spiral, vase-shaped, etc.; of particular interest on late 17th-century pieces (Plates 24, 26).

Banding. Decorative border on furniture in inlay or marquetry contrasting in colour or grain with main surface (e.g., satinwood with mahogany) (Plate 87); see also Herring-Bone Banding.

Baroque. Later (and more florid) version of Renaissance decoration seen in late Stuart carving and particularly in carved and gilt furniture of *c.*1725–50 by Kent and contemporaries (Plate 42).

Bead. Small moulding (*a*) of semicircular section on 18th-century furniture or (*b*) resembling string of beads. Bead and reel in combined round and oblong forms found as inlay in 16th century and in smaller forms in 18th.

Bentwood. Wood steamed and bent to form structural members of chairs, etc.; first developed by Thonet in Germany in early 19th century; taken up in England later, and widely developed in 20th century.

Blockboard. Modern furniture material composed of core of wood strips about one inch wide covered with fairly thick veneers.

Bolection Moulding. Ogee-shaped moulding projecting round edges of panels.

Bombé. French term for furniture with outward-swelling shape; applied particularly to English commodes in the French taste of the 18th century.

Boulle. Descriptive term for decorative inlay in metals and tortoiseshell carried out by celebrated French designer, A. C. Boulle (1642–1732). Practised in England by Gerreit Jensen at end of 17th century, and revived after 1815; 'seaweed' marquetry is a version of Boulle work.

Bracket Foot. Squared foot used from *c.*1690 on case furniture (Plates 27, 39).

Bulb. Swollen member of turned support on Elizabethan and Jacobean furniture, often with carved Ionic capital above, and with moulding of 'cup and cover' form; of Flemish origin (Plates 6, 10).

Bun Foot. Flattened ball foot introduced in late 17th century (Plate 26).

Cabochon. Convex oval ornament derived from gem; used in 16th and 17th centuries, and particularly *c.*1740 on knees of cabriole legs (Plate 43).

Cabriole Leg. Curved outwards at the knee and inwards at the foot; in general use *c.*1700–50 (Plates 27, 28, 35, 37).

Card-Cut. Ornament carved in low relief in lattice form, featured on 'Chinese' furniture of Chippendale period (Plate 53).

Cartouche. Tablet generally of oval shape with curled edges like a scroll, sometimes with inscription, arms, etc.; often found centred in broken pediments in early 18th century (Plate 41).

Caryatid. Support in form of sculptured female figure.

Cavetto. Concave moulding, quadrant of circle in profile, used prominently on cornices of furniture in walnut period (Plate 36).

Chamfer. Term for smoothed-off edge or bevelled angle (e.g., front edges of mahogany tallboys in 18th century); 'canted' and 'splayed' are similar terms (Plate 36).

Channelling. Grooves or fluting on stiles of oak furniture; also applied to grooved frames of backs of Hepplewhite period chairs (Plate 69).

Chequer. Geometrical inlay of light and dark woods found in oak furniture after *c*.1550 (Plate 9).

Chinoiserie. General term for decorative work in the Chinese taste, shown variously in japanning in 17th and 18th centuries, in Chippendale's 'Chinese' furniture, and in bamboo turning of late Georgian period.

Chipboard. Modern material made up of wood chips bonded under pressure with glues.

Chip Carving. Shallow ornament on oak furniture done with chisel and gouge (e.g., roundels on fronts of early chests) (Plate 1).

Claw-and-Ball Foot. Derived from oriental motive of dragon's claw clutching jewel or ball; celebrated terminal of early Georgian period (Plates 27, 37, 45, 50).

Club Foot. Resembling head of club; most common terminal of cabriole leg; used also with straight legs until late 18th century; when set on a disc, known as pad foot (Plates 28, 31, 43).

Cock Bead. Small astragal moulding projecting from edges of drawer fronts, much used 1730–1800 (Fig. 6, Plate 66).

Console. Bracket, normally of scroll shape; also applied to table (of French origin) supported against wall only at front by legs, or by eagle, etc., introduced in early 18th century (Plate 52).

Coquillage. Carved ornament of shell form used often in rococo period (Plates 27, 35).

Cornice. Top member of entablature—i.e., moulded projection surmounting frieze.

Cup and Cover. See Bulb.

Cupid's Bow. Term applied to curved cresting of chairs introduced *c*.1730 and prominent feature of Chippendale period (Plate 50).

Dentil. Moulding of small rectangular blocks ('teeth'), with spaces between, mainly used on cornices of mahogany furniture (Plates 79, 80).

Dolphin. Motive borrowed from France, first seen in late 17th century as terminal (arms and feet of chairs), then popularised by Kent and subsequently in Chippendale's rococo furniture.

Dowel. Wooden peg used in oak period to join timber.

Ebonised Wood. Stained black to imitate ebony; used for stringing in late Georgian period, and also for furniture in Anglo-Japanese style popularised by Godwin from *c*.1870 (Plate 114).

Egg and Dart. Classical decoration of alternating eggs and darts (said to symbolise life and death) usually carved on ovolo mouldings (Plate 41).

Egyptian Taste. Current after Napoleon's invasion of Egypt, 1798, and Nelson's victory at the Nile; manifested in sphinx head, lotus leaf, lion's head, etc., of Regency period (Plates 91, 92).

Escutcheon. Armorial shield forming centre of pediments of 18th-century furniture; also applied to ornamental metal plate surrounding keyhole.

Fielded Panel. With flat centre surrounded by bevelled edges.

Finial. Knob ornament (often vase-shaped) used on intersection of stretchers in late 17th century, and also on tops of cabinets, clock cases and pole screens (Plates 26, 33).

Fluting. Concave grooves used from 16th century onwards, but particularly on friezes and columns in late 18th century (Plates 47, 60, 64).

French Scroll. Leg terminal of outward scrolling form fashionable *c*.1750; opposite of inward turning knurl foot (Plates 54, 63).

Frets. Decorative patterns, either perforated (e.g., galleries of tea tables) or in solid (e.g., chair legs); fashionable on 'Chinese' furniture of Chippendale period.

Frieze. Horizontal section below table tops and cornices of cabinets, etc.

Gadrooning (Nulling). Carved repetitive edging of concave flutes or convex reeds, sometimes in S-form, used in oak period (e.g., on bulbs) and again from 1750 (Plate 10).

Gesso. Composition of parchment size and chalk used as base for gilding and (rarely) silvering; fashionable *c*.1690–1730 (Plate 27).

Greek Key (or Fret). See Key Pattern.

Griffin. Fabulous creature with eagle's head and wings and lion's body used occasionally as decoration on Georgian furniture.

Guilloche. Ornament of interlaced circles or ovals used on oak furniture from Elizabethan period and throughout 18th century (Plates 6, 12).

Herring-Bone Banding. Border of narrow bands of striped veneer laid obliquely together.

Hipping. Extension of cabriole leg upwards to join seat rail, found on chairs and settees *c*.1700–50 (Plate 27).

Hoof Foot. Terminal of early cabriole leg, introduced from continent in late 17th century.

Husks. Flowers strung as festoons; characteristic decoration in Adam and Hepplewhite period (Plate 69).

Key Pattern. Classical frieze ornament of repeated patterns of lines at right angles to one another, much used in Kent period (Plates 61, 93).

Knurl Foot. See French Scroll.

Laminboard. Similar to blockboard (*q.v.*) but with core of thinner strips.

Linenfold. Parchment or serviette pattern of Flemish origin used as panel decoration *c*.1480–1550.

Lion Mask. Carved decoration particularly on knees of cabriole legs *c*.1725–40 (hence the 'lion' period); revived during Regency in brass for drawer handles, as well as carved motive (Plates 40, 97).

Lotus. The 'water lily of the Nile'; fashionable decorative motive of the Egyptian taste during Regency (Plate 96).

Lozenge. Diamond-shaped panel decoration of Jacobean period (Plate 11).

Lunette. Decoration of half-moon form often found carved on later oak furniture, or inlaid and painted in Adam period (Plates 10, 11, 13).

Mitre. Intersection of moulding round panel, each edge cut at an angle of 45°.

Monopodium. Support of classical form for tables, etc., in shape of animal head and body with single leg and foot; fashionable during Regency.

Mortise. Cavity in wood to take corresponding projecting tenon to form joint (hence 'joined' furniture, joinery, joiner) (Fig. 2).

Neo-Classical. Term applied to revived classical decoration in delicate form associated with Robert Adam c.1760–90.

Ogee. Moulding of waved form, convex above, concave below.

Ormolu. Gilded metal used for furniture mounts; manufactured in England by Matthew Boulton from 1762 (Plate 59).

Ovolo. Convex moulding of quarter-circle section used on drawer fronts in late 17th century (Fig. 9).

Oyster Pieces. Small veneers of walnut, laburnum, olive, etc., cut transversely from branches and used in parquetry from 1660 (Plate 25).

Pad Foot. See Club Foot.

Palmette. Palm leaf ornament, similar to honeysuckle, like spread fan (Plate 71).

Papier-Mâché. Patent for version of this material taken out by Henry Clay in 1772 and used for furniture; but true papier-mâché furniture fashionable 1825–50 (Plate 106).

Parquetry. Geometrically-patterned veneers of oyster pieces (q.v.).

Patera. Round or oval disc decoration on furniture in the neo-classical style, carved, inlaid or painted (Plates 64, 65, 77).

Pediment. Classical triangular member surmounting cornices of cabinets, etc.; in use from 1660, but 'broken' pediments (straight, semicircular or swan-necked) popular in 18th century (Plates 41, 44).

Piecrust. Term for raised and scalloped edging of tea tables c.1750–75.

Pier. Part of room wall between windows; hence pier glass, pier table.

Pilaster. Flat column applied to cabinet, etc.

Pillar and Claw. Tripod composed of turned upright and three feet. (Plate 47).

Plinth. Foundation of carcase; plinth (or spade) foot of tapered rectangular form used in Hepple-

white period (Plates 76, 85).

Plywood. Board built up from veneers glued together, each with grain at right angles to next, giving great strength (Plate 130).

Rebate. Rectangular channel on edge of framing or of drawer (e.g., for insertion of cock bead) (Fig. 6).

Reeding. Convex raised ornament (opposite of fluting) often found on chair and table legs, etc., in later Georgian period (Plates 84, 92).

Rococo. (French *rocaille*). Form of decoration succeeding Baroque and using C and S scrolls often asymmetrically in supposed imitation of rock work; English version of furniture in this style popularised in Chippendale's *Director* (1754) (Plates 50, 52).

Romayne Decoration. Medallioned heads in profile found on early Tudor furniture as attempt at Renaissance decoration (Plate 4).

Shell. See Coquillage.

Splat. Vertical member in centre of chair back, usually shaped or pierced (Plates 27, 50).

Split Baluster. Member turned, split and applied to furniture as decoration in first half of 17th century (Plates 10, 15).

Stile. Vertical section of frame of panel into which horizontal section (rail) fitted (Fig. 2).

Strapwork. Interlaced carved geometrical bands or straps (of Flemish origin) found on furniture from c.1550.

Stretcher. Bar uniting and bracing legs of chairs, tables, etc.; usually horizontal (Plate 51), but waved shape used in late 17th century (Plate 18).

Stringing. Inlay in fine lines often found on late Georgian furniture in brass and ebonised wood (Plates 85, 88).

Tambour. Shutter or roll front of desks, etc., formed of narrow strips of wood on canvas backing, introduced in late Georgian period.

Tenon. See Mortise.

Tester. Wooden canopy over bedstead (Plate 8).

Tudor Rose. Combination of red (Lancastrian) and white (Yorkist) roses used as carved decoration on early Tudor furniture.

Vitruvian Scroll. 'Wave' pattern of convoluted scrolls found on friezes of tables, etc., particularly in Kent period, c.1725–50 (Plates 41, 42).

Windsor Chair. Traditional country 'stick-back' chair (with no known connection with Windsor), often with frame of yew or ash, legs and spindles ('sticks') of beech, and seat of ash or elm. Early 'comb-back' type followed by 'hoop-back' after c.1750; simplified versions of fashionable details often added (e.g., cabriole legs, cupid's bow cresting). Manufacture of these chairs became organised in High Wycombe from early 19th century.